SPORTS PAGES

Poetry by Arnold Adoff

Birds
Black is brown is tan
friend dog
i am the running girl
Where Wild Willie
The Poetry of Black America:
Anthology of the 20th Century

SPORTS PAGES

by Arnold Adoff

illustrations by Steve Kuzma

J. B. Lippincott   New York

Sports Pages
Text copyright © 1986 by Arnold Adoff
Illustrations copyright © 1986 by Steven Kuzma
All rights reserved. No part of this book may be
used or reproduced in any manner whatsoever without
written permission except in the case of brief quotations
embodied in critical articles and reviews. Printed in
the United States of America. For information address
J. B. Lippincott Junior Books, 10 East 53rd Street,
New York, N.Y. 10022.
4 5 6 7 8 9 10

Library of Congress Cataloging-in-Publication Data
Adoff, Arnold.
    Sports pages.

    Summary: Poems about the experiences and feelings
of young athletes involved in various sports.
    1. Sports—Juvenile poetry.   2. Children's poetry,
American.   [1. Sports—Poetry.   2. American poetry]
I. Kuzma, Steve, ill.   II. Title.
PS3551.D66S6   1986   811'.54   85-45169
ISBN 0-397-32102-3
ISBN 0-397-32103-1 (lib. bdg.)

Always for Jaime, Leigh and Title IX

I Move From Sport To Sport.

Alone in my head   during the final heat of the big race,
     or anchored in my place   as our team moves through
those final moments   between a victory   and a sad defeat:
     I move from sport to sport   as the seasons change,
                                   as we change
                           and bend and grow.

I learn.
We learn. I   know a dream can become reality.
     We know a dream can remain a dream.

Alone in my head   or taking my place   as part of a team,
     I sweat and worry.   I smile away the nagging fear.
There is always hard work, but near the end of each final
     practice session, I know I am ready to do my final
                                   best.
                     Win or lose I will do well.

I am getting stronger   the longer I play.

I am getting better each day. I can tell.

Alone In The Nets.

I

am

alone   of   course,

in the nets, on this cold and raining afternoon,

and our best defending fullback

is lying on the wet ground   out of position.

Half the opposition is pounding

down the field,

and their lead forward is gliding

so fast, she can just barely keep

the ball in front of her   sliding

foot.

Her cleats are expensive,

and her hair b$_o$u$_n$c$_e$s

neatly

like the   after
      girls   in the shampoo commercials.

There   is   a   big   grin

on her face.

9

Now: In This Frozen Moment On This Moving World Through Space

      is the right time to ask why am I here just standing

                            in my frozen place?

Why did I get up on time this morning?

Why did I get up at all?

Why did I listen to the coach and agree to play

      this strange position in a r e a l game

      in a strange town   on this wet and moving world?

Why is it raining?

Why is it raining so h a r d?

Where

      are all of our defenders?

Why do all of our players

      do all of the falling

            down?

           Why am I here?

But Frozen Moments Can Unfreeze And I Can Stretch

and reach for the ball   flying to the corner of

                                                   our

                                               goal.

I can reach   and jump
         and dive   into the s p a c e

                 between my out
                    stretched
                       hands

and the outside poles

       of the nets.

My fears evaporate   like my sweat in this chilling

                                breeze,

and I can move with this moving world

and pace my steps

like that   old
        movie

      high
      noon   sheriff   in his just

              right

              time.

That grinning forward gets her shot away too soon,
and I am there, on my own time, in the air,
                                    to meet the ball,
and fall on it
for   the save.

I wave my happy ending wave and get up.
                    The game   goes on.

Watch Me On The Wing.

Sweeper: the deeper I can play
        the faster I can lay
out my traps for their fullback
moving too close to mid   field.
I shine along the side   lines
        from mid   field
        back to our goal.

I am the quickest,
        sharpest,
most   intelligent,
(and
most m o d e s t ,) player on
             my
           team:
      in this league.

I have the

superspeed:

I have the need to do a little

                          more

than play only one position. I

defend. I score. I run like

                          wind

across the corn fields   of

                          this

                          town.

I am a brown tornado on a

                          muddy

                          day.

The opposition knows

I come to play   with

all I bring. They

                  watch:

w a t c h   m e   o n   t h e   w i n g .

Prohibited Acts: Attacking From The Rear. Kicking.   Tripping.

Hitting   or

punching.

Holding.   Pushing.

Roughness.

Using the hands or

arms

intentionally.

Dangerous or wild

play.

Interference.

Blocking with the

shoulder. Kicking

the   ball from the

goalie's hands.

Illegally

attacking

the goalie.

Attacking

the

goalie.

Though The Afternoon Was Freezing Cold,

there was a place
in front of the
                  nets
that was soft and
         dug out.

When the cleats
on my right foot
caught in that
         soft
              mud,
my body was
already turning
and following
into the play.
My right knee
              was
         turning
              too.

Only my foot
remained
      unmoving
in its   unmoving
        shoe.

This was   definitely   not   a good   day.

My Knee Is Only Sprained,

                is   only   swollen,
and
the doctor says   I will be
                       fine.
           I'll play again.

           He says this as he
           sits   on his padded
           leather chair that
           can swivel 360 de
                 grees.
           Oh
              why can't knees?

Still.   We do not make the Six O'Clock News
           with this old story, often told, of
                pain and frustration and fear.
Still.
        I must sit on this bench and be as
still as this brace demands;
        as
still as the other spectators behind me in
                       the stands.
I have been told: next season,
                next y e ar.

Wrestling The Beast.

This guy is an animal. A pig?   Squealing sinus breathing.

A bear?   Hair on his fat arms.

A dog?   No, not biting, but his

chin

digging into my collar

bone.

A dragon.   Easy. Dragon breath.

An anaconda snake. His mistake:

choke hold around my neck.

A jackal? A hyena? A hungry lion?

A wounded   tiger

alone in the dark bush?

A bee?

An

ant? A worm? A toad? A dying fly on the end of a frog's

tongue?

This guy is an animal. A gentle cat rolled

over

by me.

O n e.

T w o.

Three.

Coach Says: Listen Sonny, You Are The Safety On This Team,
And Your Body Belongs To Me, And Your Safety Is The Last
Thing On Your Mind. Right? Right. Their Guy Is Super Fast.
Do Not Let Him Get Past. Period. Understood? Safety Last.
Now Play It By The Numbers.

Simple.

    We start with eleven when the whistle blows,

and

       their quarterback throws his pass.

                 Simple.

Number One: He throws the ball.

Number Two: The ball is caught.

Number Three: Their receiver runs

         d o w n the field

             toward me.

Number Four

Through Ten: My team

        mates who ought to stop him are hit

    or

      fall, or miss, or are too slow to make

              the play.

Simple.

    Safety last. I am the last of our eleven,

      and the runner runs my way.

Afternoons: One.

The way I am playing this position, I must look like a full back
with half a brain. I am too slow. I need a heatrub fix. I am far
beyond some green water and a heavily advertised candy bar. Even
though I tend to exaggerate during emotional situations, this is
the crucial last long moment of this crucial game.

Just when I need that just right word, or clear fact of strategy
that might help me get past their monster tackle and lug the ball
into the endzone of victory and personal glory, I look toward my
bench and blink: I see coach turn his back on me.

Oh

please forgive this bitter moment of mine as my
face disappears into the mud of the one yard line.

Afternoons: Two.

No one owns
a foot ball
on   this
            street.
We roll the
morning
            paper
and
tie it with
            old
                rope
and
hope it
            holds
through the
tough
passing
game.

When you catch my pass   you tuck this paper
in your gut   and make your feet deliver the
                                    winning news.

Afternoons: Three.

On the FourthOfJuly
up
on the town
            hill   there
                        are
swimming
      and
diving
            races   and
                        a
bike rodeo around
                        the
                        park.

We have to
run
red markers through
a safety course and
clock our times. We
play catch and sack
              race
and   learn
         a
      batch of games
where
      no one loses
      no one wins.
We
pop our wheelies un
              til
       dark.

Point Guard.

You bring the ball down the court.
The pick is set.
The play is set. The movement of
the ball
is faster
than all
the
defensive
hands and heads,
and you
get free.

You pass into the big girl
at the key. She turns
and
shoots and scores.

The crowd roars.

33

Sweet.

You are at the line. You take a deep breath.
                      You take a deep breath.

You know: a free   throw
                      is really
      a   free   throw:
                    no hands in your face;
                    no race   down
                                    the court;
                    no block,
                    no clock.

This is the place   to score. This is the time to pour   it in,
        and beat those   nasty bad guys   on the   other   team,
                                    once   and   for   all.
This is the time to win   this   game.

You bounce the ball once, and wish   for all the luck
                    you know   you   don't need.
You shoot,   and the ball
            flies
                  and   arcs   and speeds   down   through
                    the hoop   to meet the net.

You get   your point; your score; your wish.   Swish.

Sweet.

My
Short
Story.

I just can't shoot over the shoulders   and arms and hands
of this monster-with-a-smile who is their center tonight.
He swats my shots like so many slow motion flies floating
near his head. My dunk is dead. He is too tall. Period.

  He

is a wall of meat in short pants. I just know he must

                                    shave

                    after   every   meal:

                    six   times   a   day.

How can the refs let him play

against   my   short-legged   self?

I feel   like   some   Santa's   elf.

My

sweet jump

        shot   hits him   in   the numbers

                        on   his   chest.

                    How do   you   drive around

                    an   18-wheeling   semi   for

                    a   lay   up   shot?   You

                                        do

                                        not

                                        !

I just can't pass this test

                    this

                        game.

I just   can't   shoot.

I just   can't   score.

My

short

story   is   a   bore.

Afternoons: Four.

Milkshake with eggs:
my legs up on the
          table
as the screen shows
slow motion secrets
of my favorite pros.
I dream with o p e n
        e y e s
my future d r e a m:
the new K a r e e m.

Even The Light Seems Dark

as it comes in through the dirty windows of the gym.
The afternoon is darkening into evening, and I am
                               still at work at these machines:
lifting and pulling
t h e s e   weights until   my shirt is dark   with   sweat.

Then: I get up from the mats and run

       up and down the school stairs: first floor to third,

                      third floor to first,

     over and over and over again.

Then: I do road running and stretching and road running,

   again

   until true

       dark and the pale moon begins to r i s e.

Then. Look: no surprise. I am getting stronger,

                 am stronger.

                 Strong.

    You want to see muscle:

       here is muscle.

    You want to see leg:

       here is leg.

Now I think it's time to bend this toughened knee,

and b e g the coach to let me play on Saturday.

My Team Without Me.

Rough turf,

or an icy surface

        patch

on some strange

        field,

and I can twist

my ankle just
            like
            that.

Or a cheap hit

(from my blind

        side,)

can knock

me flat and

        r i p

my

      last good knee.

And I will sit on benches

through the longest games

in darkening afternoons,

that I have ever had to

    stay seated through,

    and

        only

      see.

43

Exercises: To Be Done Each Day.

1. 30 jumping jacks.
2. 10 windmills.
3. 5 leg crossovers: each leg.
4. 25 leg switches: mountain climbing.
5. 10 hamstring pulls.
6. Trunk rotations.
7. 8 push-ups.
8. 30 sit-ups.
9. Hurdle-stretches.
10. 20 toe-risers.
11. Arm circles.
12. Neck rotations.

Week Before A Monday Meet:

Sunday And Wednesday.   Exercises.

Jog 4 minutes. Run 6 minutes at 1/2 speed.

Walk 2 minutes. Repeat 2 times.

Run 3 minutes at 3/4 speed.

Walk 2 minutes. Repeat 3 times.

Run 60 seconds: hard.

Walk 60 seconds. Repeat 2 times.

Run 5–10 minutes.

Sprint at end.

Jog 6 minutes to cool down.

Monday And Thursday.   Exercises.

Jog 4 minutes: easy.

Run 10 minutes: nonstop. Walk 3 minutes.

Run 60 seconds at 3/4 speed.

                  Walk 60 seconds.

                  Repeat 4 times.

Run 5 minutes as hard as you can.

Jog 6 minutes to cool down.

Tuesday And Friday.   Exercises. Jog 5 minutes: easy.

Run 4 minutes at 3/4 speed.

Jog 4 minutes: nonstop. Repeat 3 times.

Run 45 seconds. Walk 60 seconds.

                  Repeat 4 times.

Run 8 minutes: nonstop. Sprint at end.

Jog 6 minutes to cool down.

Saturday. Warm up. Exercises. Run 20 minutes: nonstop.

Sunday. R e l a x. E a t i c e c r e a m.

YOU

                begin to run
                        when
SHE   is almost up
                            to
YOU.

YOU   are both moving.
YOU   are staying in
                        your
                    l a n e .
YOU   are picking up
                        speed.

SHE   is stretching
                            to
reach your
                    retreating
                        back,
                        and

YOU need
to stretch your
left arm back,
and feel her
smack that baton
into the palm
of your hand,
and

YOU are
off as
fast
as
YOU can sprint.

Afternoons: Five.

On saturday afternoons the downtown community center
gets free   passes to SkateWorld. We spend the d a y
playing   crack the whip   and tag   and bragging   back
                                                                            ward
to the heavy metal beat. Our feet flash
                                        in mirrored
                                            lights.

Mixed Singles.

She tosses the tennis ball   high

                              into   the   air.

Her

racket comes down harder than I   e v e r

                                          k n e w

a

racket could hit.

It

is a serve into the inside corner,

that I barely see: kicking   chalk

as

it flies away, untouched   by   me

I know this will be love.

53

Ground

Bound

I

watch:

I hold

my

breath

for

my

bend

ing

friend

on

the

par

all

els.

Even

when I

spot

here

from

this

side I

take

this

balance

r
 i
  d
   e
    .

Dear Horse:

          you want this apple.

        and I

           want that

            competition cup.

You

know how to hold your head

          up   straight.

I

know how to post so right,

I could hold a glass

of water in my hand

and not spill a drop.

Please watch out for pheasants

flying up under your nose. Don't

get thirsty just yet. Keep

          rabbits off

        y o u r toes.

D o n ' t

s t o p.

57

Last Frame

of
this game called
                slow
                pitch:
and
I
whip   that
       ball   sofast,
             even
             under
             hand,

her   bat

is much

       too

late

     to meet   my

          throw

across   the   plate.

Third strike.

Third o u t .

I

love that l a s t

        great

        shout.

Last   frame.

End of game.

There Is A Very Ugly

bruise
on the right
      side   of   my
      right
        knee;
and
an o ther very ug
           ug
             ugly
bruise
on the right
      side   of   my
      right
        arm;
but the
      charm bracelet on my wrist shines new
      and sweet as I sip my soda and smile
      into a certain pair of BigBrown eyes
            this friday afternoon.

What a great time to be a g i r l.

These Knees:

these joints: these soft and floating combinations
                of cartilage and ligament and bone:
these knees

                were

                made   to bend and flex and

                                        run

                the power of thigh and

                                leg

                                muscles

                                together,

                at the instant

                of the   starting

                                gun.

These knees were never made to be hit by shoulder pads,
                or helmets, or the f l y

                                        i n g   bodies   of

                                        young   heroes,

                                        and   heroines:

                impressing   home

                                town

                                fans.

Equal Curses On Two Long Lines Of Equally Short Ancestors.

Because I am so short, I will crouch down at the plate

and

bend my knees, and try to fool the umpire,

to fool the pitcher

into pitching pitches

outside,

so I can get on base.

Equal curses on that giant of a pitcher,

and his own long lines of ancestors.

Because I am so short, I hate to swing that bat   and miss.

I hate to strike out   and   listen

to my team

mates   groan   and

shout.

I want to run and hide.

If the ball comes close inside, I won't jump
away.
I stay within
my crouch,
even
if it hits my
knee.

Equal curses on ancestors and pitchers
and pitches and
on
me.

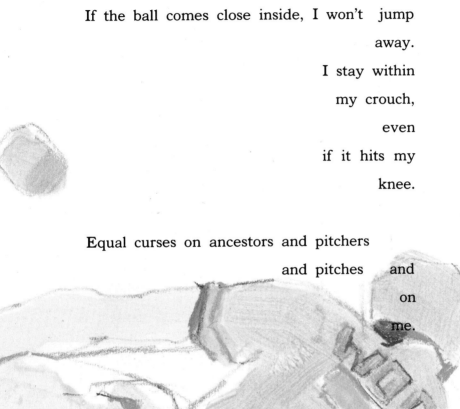

65

One Finger   Along The Seam Of The Ball,

or

one finger   across the seam of the ball.   Either way
you

will be throwing fast balls.
Strikes:
time after time.

Remember: it is in the speed,
or

in taking   a
little

off

the speed.

Throw straight. Don't aim. Try and throw the   same
way

time after time.

Think of the flapping of wings   through   the   air,
or things with fins
moving through   water
the way the   ball moves through   air.

We always need the wins but your   elbow

is much too

young

for the   curve.

Catcher.

I am always heavy. This mask is pulling down my head.
This chest protector feels like some kind of concrete
ball deflector.

These shin guards slow my running
Toward first with the faked throw.   I am always late to

            the back stop,

        to chase foul balls

        for easy outs.

All my movements are short and heavy behind the plate.
I am the battery mate for the pitcher. I signal the

        pitcher. I signal the

        pitch;   signal

            w h i c h

infielder will move behind

        second
    for the pick o f f
        play.

I am always heavy
in my heavy crouch. But when that slick runner comes on
in from third, and I have the ball in my mitt, waiting
for his heavy hit,
I am the catcher: rooted to the ground for all it takes.
I hold on to the ball and make the out.

Being heavy is what it's all about.

My Left Foot Is Always   Near The Bag.

First base. I am ready with my glove
to field grounders, or

hard

hit

line drives.
I am ready
to take the throw and

step

on

first

base

to   get   the   runner   o u t.

I am ready to put the

tag

on
an ankle or foot or toe,
and hold on to the ball
and not let go   until

the

umpire's

shout.

My left foot is always   near the bag.

I Am The Best Second
           Base Person

                              on this team, but I play short
                                                        stop,
                              because my arm   is better than
                              any
                              of our   other player's   best.
                              You know
                                        the
                                        other
                              teams have put it to the test.

I can burn my throws straight to first,
and light up the hand
                        inside that first
                                    base
                                    man's
                                    glove.
I love it   when the guy yells:
                        OW!
GOOD THROW!

I know
    that
    loud
respect.

Sometimes In Center Field On A Hot Summer Evening,

when the air is so still   you almost think you hear
                the mosquitos warming up their engines,
and
our pitcher is getting
the o p p o s i t i o n
to dribble grounders
        to the infield.
                .
              . .

Sometimes   in center field
I have a hard time staying
                awake.
I never
    close my eyes and fall asleep standing,
            but my mind will m o v e
                            o v e r
to last week's extra-inning loss
and my wild toss to third to
                help
them score and help *us* lose that g a m e.

My throat is always too dry
and there is always an ice
                    cold
                    can
of pop waiting at the   cold
                    pop
                    stand.

One time   a well-hit ball   popped into my outstretched hand
                    before I could remember   my name.

Two

Out   In The Bottom Of The Ninth,

and this is the s l o w m o t i o n   part of the movie.
I
am in the movie, near the end of a long game.
the announcer is calling my name.   The fans are calling
                        my name.   The ball is   flying
                        s l o w l y   over my head   as
I run s l o w l y
            u n d e r it: catch up with it at the far fence.

In this moment of s l o w suspense   no one knows how it
                                    will all come out.
The announcer and the fans and
                        the
    coach all wait.
    The hitter waits.
                I wait too.
But
my feet have left the ground   and my arm   is stretching
                    higher than the flying ball.

76

Then it is all over, and the movie moves ahead: the

                                                    b a l l

        is in my glove, and I am s i t t i n g on

                                        the out

                                        f i e l d

                                        green.

The game is over, and I imagine   my name

heads the credits spread across s o m e

            imaginary

                        s c r e e n .

We   Have   Our   Moments.

Sometimes   we leap and land.
Sometimes   we t r i p and f a l l.
Sometimes   we catch the other team   before they score.
Sometimes   we jump too soon   and get faked out of our

socks.

We can be sharp on the pick-off play at third.
Or

we can have rocks in our heads and miss that

softly batted ball,

and miss that

one

sweet   chance   to

save

the

day.

I lose. I win. We lose. We win.
The team   finishes   in last place.
The team is

in the play-offs at last

and past defeats f a d e

fast.

We   have   our   moments.

Arnold Adoff is the winner of the 1988 National Council of Teachers of English Award for Excellence in Poetry for Children. He was born and educated in New York City, and was a teacher there for twelve years. Mr. Adoff is the distinguished editor of nine anthologies of American poetry and prose, including I AM THE DARKER BROTHER and THE POETRY OF BLACK AMERICA. He is the author of fifteen award-winning collections of poetry for young readers including BLACK IS BROWN IS TAN, EATS: POEMS, and I AM THE RUNNING GIRL. He is the husband of noted author Virginia Hamilton; and their two children, Leigh Hamilton and Jaime Levi, provided much of the inspiration for these sports poems. Mr. Adoff travels widely, working with young authors and their adult friends.

Steve Kuzma enjoys many sports, and his favorites are soccer and skiing. As an active participator in these sports, he is especially sensitive to athletes' emotions during training and competition. He sees sports as an all-important part of the development of mind, body, and spirit together. He is a graduate of Parsons School of Design. His work has appeared in *The New York Times* and on CBS, SIN Television promoting the '85 World Cup, and ABC's coverage of the 1984 Winter Olympics in Sarajevo and the 1984 Summer Olympics in Los Angeles.